The Sense of Place

David Singleton

Grosvenor House
Publishing Limited

This book is published by
Grosvenor House Publishing Ltd
28-30 High Street, Guildford, Surrey, GU1 3EL.
www.grosvenorhousepublishing.co.uk

A CIP record for this book
is available from the British Library

ISBN 978-1-78148-355-8

Palazzola

Some of these poems are about events, or encounters. Some of them might, years ago, have caused me pain or embarrassment. Now, they mostly amuse me. I hope readers may share that amusement. More of them, however, are about places. I live on the edge of the West Pennines, and these low hills, these dark, claggy fields, these sudden shafts of sunlight through parted clouds haunt my imagination. Many of the poems reflect this. Others are about places I have merely visited, but which remain with me. Usually, these are places, like Arctic Norway or the Hebrides that have a sense of being at the edge of the world. Palazzola, however, is not like this.

I suppose there are still relatively few people who know about Palazzola. I do not wish to change that. Really, I want to keep the place to myself. Only the fact that very few people will read this book induces me to begin with a description of the place. Do not therefore imagine that I recommend it. It is not for everyone: only for those who value peace, quiet, seriousness and an atmosphere of study and prayer. I do not myself pray, nor do I believe in the efficacy of prayer, but I am happy to be in the company of those who do. You meet a lot of people like me at Palazzola. I hope that will deter the casual visitor. "Procul, O procul este, profani," as we say in Wigan.

Palazzola is in the Castelli Romani, south-west of Roman, far enough away from the city to have a rural feel and close enough for a day in Rome to be easily arranged. If you are wise, you fly into Rome's lesser airport, Ciampino, which is both much closer and much less obnoxious than Fiumicino. You are then driven along pleasant country roads until, after about ten minutes you turn right and climb steeply past the Alban Lake towards the hill town of Rocca di Papa. Rocca di Papa is only about two thousand feet above sea-level, but the sea is, after all, not very far away and the town towers sufficiently impressively over the Plain of Latium to have an Alpine feel.

Palazzola is about a mile from the centre of Rocca di Papa, but entirely cut off from it by a mountain road of such frenzied busyness that to attempt to cross it on foot would be to risk death and to affront the manhood of the drivers who scream past at improbable speeds. A narrow, stone-flagged drive, skirting an immense wall takes you down to Palazzola itself. You pull up in a small courtyard at the door of what appears to be a monastery.

And that indeed is what it is. Palazzola is, or was, a thirteenth century Cistercian house, and it feels like one. The Cistercians had a preference for remoteness. Here, they had the best of both worlds: Palazzola is secluded, but actually not very far away from civilisation. It overlooks the Alban Lake itself and there, across the water, reflected in the water, is Castelgandolfo, currently neglected by Pope Francis but still a sight to wonder at. Nevertheless, the house itself feels like a mountain refuge: the only access to it, other than from the drive, is from a narrow footpath that winds along the steep and densely wooded slopes overlooking the lake. Or used to: the footpath was washed away in the heavy rains of the autumn of 2013 and has not yet been restored. When I return, I shall not therefore see the mules, bells ringing, that occasionally came up the path carrying firewood for the ovens and the fireplace in the library.

You can hide in those woods. The story is that the grandfather of the current director did so from the Nazis, leaping from the terrace wall to make his escape. You can lose yourself in these woods. I have done so, attempting to walk to Nemi and emerging somewhere unidentifiable to me, but thoughtfully provided with an excellent restaurant. Nemi! If I could live anywhere, I might live in Nemi and eat only the delicious wild strawberries and drink only the fragrant local Frascati. It is a place of mystery, with a grinning crucifix in the local church and a volcanic lake (the Speculum Dianae), connected to Lake Albano by a subterranean passage, fringed by thick woods through which a young priest once dashed, in deadly fear, pursued by his licensed killer and successor as Rex Nemorensis. There is a street in the town named after the author of "The Golden Bough."

The Convento di Palazzola belongs to the English College in Rome. It is therefore principally a place of study for seminarians, but it is available to others for study, prayer, retreat, or just for a holiday. It is not a place for sybarites; the rooms still have a monastic feel to them, but the food is good and copious and the wine flows freely. There is a terrace with a view over the lake and beyond, looking towards the sea, somewhere near Ostia; the towers and domes of Rome itself are visible, glinting in the sun on a clear day. There are invariably interesting people to meet: people, usually, who take life, if not themselves, seriously. The library smells deliciously of woodsmoke and is as good a place as I know to while away a day thinking and reading. The nights are quiet, country-dark and haunted by owls.

I go to Palazzola once a year, usually in the company of my wife and our friends, David and Patsy Hinchliffe, and I have shared with them many of the places referred to in this book, all of them enhanced by their good humour, enthusiasm and perceptiveness. David's painting of Palazzola appears on the cover of this book, which is a poor repayment for a great friendship, but it is dedicated to them, as well as to Palazzola itself.

To David and Patsy Hinchliffe

Contents

Page

Palazzola

Nemi

We go to eat the strawberries:

Precise and sweet and fragrant

Under the melting cream. Nearby,

Caligula looks with manic eyes

Beyond the buildings, towards the lake.

An occasional passing tourist

Thinks to himself or says that now

Is the time to read the Golden Bough.

I first saw Nemi late one day

As darkness fell upon the afternoon

And on the forests around the lake:

Deep, volcanic, numinous and black.

The high-piled buildings seemed to form

An imminent avalanche,

Across the lake I saw the gleam

Of carlights descending, as in a dream.

We ate our strawberries,

And sipped a sweet white wine:

The sort you sip your biscuits in.

A crucifix with a sickly grin,

Carved of cypresses

In the unprepossessing church

Made us shrink, and think that now

Might be the time to read the Golden Bough.

Palazzola

We will meet again, I hope, next year

Here, above the cypresses

And umbrella pines, here

On the terrace, by the lake

Which is for us a mirror

Of life spent usefully.

Did you hear the owl this morning

Early, in the trees, calling

The world to witness

And wakefulness

As the sun rolled the dark

Away, and with it doubt?

The Path has Gone

Cypresses, lizards and umbrella pines,

Sun and the song of birds, laughter

Of women in the Fra Angelico sky

Mirrored in unruffled waters: spring

In Italy, the Alban Hills falling

To the plain of Latium in a green flood.

The path has gone. In November

It was there, disciplining the rough hill.

Rain undercut it, scooping out the earth,

Sending the stone, scattering, showering

Down into the dark water, unreflecting,

Unfathomable. There is no trail winding,

Weaving as in a kind of lattice the thick wood;

There is no path to the umbrella pine,

No way to penetrate the deepening

Dark; no walking to Castelgandolfo,

No brief, circuitous pilgrimages.

Who will restore it, shore up the sides,

Set limits to the falling away

Of earth, restore our faith?

No one knows who has the will,

The vision or the power, here

In forests where the spirit of the year

Was seen to run screaming and afraid.

Passing at Palazzola

This would be a good place, if there can be

A good place, to die: unnoticed, quietly

In the sun, by the wall, where the wisteria

Flowers, to the accompaniment of the bee,

The murmuring on the terrace, the blinding sea

Away off, the evening imperceptibly

Darkening. A good place. A good time.

No fuss. No drama. Drawn into the sublime

Like Ganymede, gently, unobtrusively,

No embarrassed travesty of goodbye,

Only the failure to hear the dinner bell

To signal passing, an orison, a knell

By simple accident of being there

Dying politely in the insect-dappled air.

Sun

Sunlight came slowly in the garden,

Rising over the cliff face

Of the bishop's wall, filling the terrace,

Where we sat, with sudden animation.

Men stripped off their sweaters,

Women laid their coloured shawls aside,

Birds celebrated the epiphany aloud

In the haphazard geometry

Of the covered walk, the tangled trees.

The sun came up. We sipped our tea,

And thought we might walk the Appian Way

Today, tomorrow, under the umbrella pines,

Between the tombs, regulated by cypresses,

The stones, the rambling skeletons

Of ancient aqueducts, portentous tombs,

Theatres, circuses, flickering lizards

Born in the crevices of broken ashlar

Cast there by forgotten catastrophes;

And under all, stacked as in supermarket shelves,

The sardonic skeletons of ordinary saints.

Northern Places

The North

This is the landscape that I love;

The country that possesses me.

It has baptised me with its rain,

Set over me a canopy of cloud,

Anointed me with its sunshine,

Shriven me with its cold,

Tormented me with its heat.

It has received me when I fall,

Nurtured me in its soft earth.

When I have risen, it has borne me,

Lifted me to its heights,

Followed me to its depths,

Cast a resemblance of me

In the still waters of its lakes,

And by the music of its rivers

Accompanied my song,

Comforted my grief.

And when I ache from climbing

I have slept in the comfort

Of its grass. It belongs

To me, and I to it,

By bonds deeper than love,

More permanent than faith.

A Meeting by the Reservoir

March it is, and raining:

Insistent, but not hard,

Gently initiating

A quiet conversation

With the leafless branches

Of lifeless trees,

Vainly clutching, catching

At the falling sky

With fractal geometry

Impromptu tracery,

Ribs without vaults.

The path is oozy black,

A dark and stinking mousse,

Clinging, claggy, clayey,

Sliding, slithering

Pounded by thousands:

Feet, rubber –ramparted;

Wheels of bike, patterned

With grooves, criss-cross,

Or parallel, horses

Fertilizing the earth

With their own fragrance.

From far off, I see them,

Shuffling in a line,

Not quite a column,

Grey-black in hooded

Anoraks, armoured

Against the rain, risen

From the earth: mud-men,

Loam men, soil-men,

Men of mire, and ooze

And clinging clay,

Men lumpen, limping.

As they draw more near

I see them for what they are;

I see that they are mad men,

Led men, escorted

For an outing, along

The gluey path, beside

The grey water, under

The low-slung sky:

Black men are with them,

Strong, hard muscles;

Without asking, I know why.

Suddenly, a limping,

Lumpen figure

Tilts back his head

And offers to the sky

A sudden paroxysm

Of hate or anger

Addressed to nothing,

Addressed to everything,

Then sinks back again

Into sedated silence

And passes quietly by.

A sort of chill seeps in,

As in the presence

Of some perverted sacrament,

Some parody,

Odious and pitiable,

Instantly recognized,

Yet utterly strange.

"There," we say, "but for

The Grace of God," but

If this, too, is not the grace

Of God, what shall we ascribe it to?

A Wet Day

Lancashire was grey today;

Somewhere over Cheshire, there was blue,

But the wind chased it all away,

And invited the rain in, too.

It held the door in the sky ajar

And let the rain come bustling in,

And the hills so grey, so far,

Withdrew, as the sky fell in.

And the wind told its ancient lie

Of a tomorrow better than today,

But the clouds came scudding by

And folded the sunshine in.

Above Rivington

The rhododendrons are not on fire

In the Japanese garden, under the hill;

Spring has not yet kindled them,

Not set the torch to mangled roots,

Not ignited the month-long flame

That will give a borrowed glamour

To the sodden grass, the peaty soil

Haphazard stones, teetering waterfalls,

Ravines, and winter-swollen streams,

And make them in April, going

Into May, faintly, farcically, tropical.

Now, there are only dogs, diving

Into the pond in hopeless loud pursuit

Of scarcely troubled ducks, and men,

Brightly-coated, worried about their weight,

Seating in the unexpected sun.

At Loch Coruisk

We are here now, but are not needed

Here, our presence as unnoticed

As inessential. Like great boulders

Laid on stones, the seals incuriously

Watch our passing by, saluting

Indifferently our insignificance.

Nothing but the cold and glittering sea,

The cloud-snagging pinnacles

Rising from the loch, the bright

And distant islands under

The everlasting, ever-changing sky;

Nothing but these matter, nothing

Else belongs. The sea-eagle eyes

Us with the contempt he has

For all that is not prey, knowing

That we are not here to stay.

Remember the North

Decaying cities, rolling moors,

Smell of peat, call of curlew,

Sting of hail on reddened cheeks,

West wind off the sea, lines

Of anoraks at football grounds,

Children bent into the wind,

Dragged like shopping trolleys

By harassed mums. Above,

Beyond the lines of terraces,

A distant haze of heather,

Buzzards in their leisurely

Orbits, sheep disciplining

The fell: the North, forgotten

By those who can, managed

In decline, like a patient

In a hospice, having nothing

Else to do, except to die.

Cartmel

Eighteenth century houses, round a square,

A priory church massively presiding there:

People loitering in the sudden blaze of spring,

Hills bland with sunshine, disbelieving

Birds clucking in alarm. Early March

And a shadow sharp under the high arch

That guards the entrance to the ginnel

Winding a deeply shadowed tunnel

Between high fronts, decorous and austere,

Of small-windowed houses rising sheer

And abrupt from neatly cobbled stones.

And in the Priory yard, contented bones,

Carved names obliterated by time,

Rain, wind, the long-accumulated

Slime of lichen, under the smooth lawn,

Tidied by industrious sheep, soon to be shorn.

On High Cup Nick

Often there is only, lonely, me:
A pony may graze incuriously
A hill away, or a buzzard stir the sky
In stately revolutions, portentously,
But often, there is only me
To contemplate the mystery.

Nowhere else so challenges me,
Assaults my incredulity,
So tempts me out of unconviction,
Almost elicits an affirmation
That someone must have made
The wonder that is here displayed.

Such perfect symmetry,
Exquisite geometry,
Created, in the absence of design,

By accident, the fortuitously benign

Sculpting of soil and scree

By rock and ice and infinity.

Often, there is only, lonely, me,

And time to accompany me:

An age, a moment to sit and stare

High in the chilled, west-facing air.

Away from the pony's incurious gaze,

While above, the buzzards laze.

Walking in the North Pennines

This is yours, this world,

This emptiness of sour fields,

Peat fastnesses, sheep.

Crumbling drystone walls,

Broken skies, shaven hills,

Sudden ascents of larks,

Callings of curlews,

Whimpering buzzards,

Sailing clouds, shadowing

Fields of waving grass,

Chilling air, aching heights,

Steep, stony pathways,

Sliding scree, mud

Sucking at sore feet.

This is yours. No one

Else wants this, not today.

You walk alone, over

Dufton, Marton,

Hilton or Appleby,

And all the world

Has gone away, leaving

This lovely emptiness.

Ness

Ness is closed on Tuesdays.

The azaleas must burn alone,

The rhododendrons flame unseen,

One day in their brief season,

While the hanging cherries

Drip pink and white confetti

On the sodden grass. Ness

Is closed, and out on the sea,

The anvil clouds march in

Towards the estuary; the gulls,

Driven like falling petals,

Fly for shelter in, and all

Unseen, the drama

Of the dying season playing

To an empty house.

Hebrides

Wedgwood-blue waters undisturbed

On white sands, sea glistening

In island-interrupted distances,

Sober mountains, dark cliffs

Rising out of sea locks, ripples

That might be otters, shadows

On surfaces that might be seals,

Far-off specks that may be eagles;

Sun breaking through cloud,

Cloud gathering, stifling light;

Whales somewhere in the sound

You never see, but memory

Says that they are there, away

Off beyond the great drumming

Of driven waters on drenched

Rocks, where you cannot see.

And everywhere the pulse

Of loneliness, everywhere the ache

Of a million hearts elsewhere,

Buried beyond the sea.

On Winter Hill

On Winter Hill, the wind is never-failing,

A companion, faithful in its way,

Though not, like Pylades, silent

And not, like Achates, a friend

Engaged to fill a hexameter:

Always there, shrill and insistent,

Or gentle, rustling the soft rush

Or bending the sedge over

The lark's nest. It will always

Be there, long after our moment

Has gone, scattered like the blown leaf

Or the wisp of smoke that sometimes

In summer rises from scorched earth

And is gone. Above, the raven

Batters at the gale, then yields,

Raised like a standard over

An unseen hoste, the curlew's cry

Is limp with distance; the grouse,

Disturbed, breaks out its startled

Rattle, sardonic and alarmed.

Midsummer on Thornton Beach

Midsummer's day: bright and blue,

Old ladies sitting by the sea, parked

In cars with open windows, watching

The receding tide, clouds as small

As gulls scudding across the sand,

Impossibly manicured and flat,

Stretching to the far-off hills,

Small children squealing far away

Where the water nipped their toes,

Dogs in the grip of madness:

Exhilarated by space and absence

Of inhibition, scampering

In pointless, crazy circles, celebrant,

Unknowing, at the solstice.

Inland, the prissy villages

Close their streets, hang flowers

On men's hats, bells on hands

And feet, breaking the silence

Of the summer afternoon

With the music of the pipe

And tambourine, and the battering

Rhythm of dancing feet. Somewhere

In the woods a half-remembered figure

Waits to be evoked, summoned to the feast.

But here, there is only sky and sea

And distant figures and skimming birds

And all the purity of emptiness.

Seals

Blank, black, guileless eyes,

Bodies bulky, sleek,

Attempting to be fish,

Helpless, harmless,

Mindless, timeless,

The moving water

The passing clouds

The curious boats

Reflected in eyes

Unwavering, unmeaning:

Beyond, unseen,

The mountains leaping

From the sea, islands

Strung in brilliance,

Gulls and gannets,

Eagles straddling

Currents of air.

Only the immemorial

Rock, the dark surface

For these that watch

And do not see

Resting on the Moors

Cold air, they say, is on its way,

Viking air, spare, austere, bladed,

Cutting and precise. A chill day

For late August, the heather on the hill

Celebrates the early chill.

I could imagine myself alone.

Lying beside a drystone wall

Out on the moor, quiet as a stone,

Watching clouds, obese and gray,

Hiding the summer away.

The merlin must be on the wing,

For no bird is moving,

And there is none that sing.

From their absence, from that silence,

Unseen, I infer her influence.

I think that if I were to die

Here, gazing at the clouds,

I could contented lie,

Like the forgotten carcasse of a sheep

Tuning the Northern wind, asleep.

The Rivington word square

It is an old church, made to look old,
Grown older, sandstone weathering
In the rain; rain was invented here
In Lancashire, along with smoke,
And paints stone walls grey, then black,
Eating surfaces away as years leak
From the nipple of eternity.

It stands above the reservoir,
Discrete in an encircling wood,
Next to a green on which the click
Of bowl on jack and the muttered oaths
Of elderly men struggling to bend
At indiscernible waists populate
The summer nights, while swallows
Skim improbable impromptu curves.

One grave draws my curiosity

Among the indistinguishable stones:

A child, a little girl, dead these thirty years,

The grave larger than the rest, made ready

For those yet to follow her. Behind

The stone, gold on black marble,

A square of words, unmeaning in themselves,

Signifying faith to those who hold their key.

A Christian anagram from days

Of martyrdom, concealment, gatherings

In the dank gloom of catacombs,

Signifying faith, initiation, fear

And hope. Here, in a wooded hill

In Lancashire, what can it mean?

What, perhaps, it always did: a dark

Reality, lit by illusion, a hope snatched.

Remember?

Do you remember Lancashire?
It used to be, more or less, here:
Cobbled streets, clogs, rainy skies,
Red-cheeked girls with solid thighs,
Saucy postcards, Blackpool, Belle Vue,
Fish and chips, tripe, footballers who
Looked middle-aged at twenty-three,
Wearing bloomers down to the knee.

It's all gone now; when HS2
Arrives, it will be forgotten too.
Lancashire was cancelled in 1983,
Without notice to you or me;
Good job we're all soft in the head,
And haven't noticed we are dead.

Ego sum Polydorus

Two workmen were killed in Ypres by an unexploded shell
from the Great War

It is the grip of Polydorus

From beneath the earth, unburied,

The grasp of bony fingers clutching

At the passing life, blood, movement,

Warmth, light, unarticulated fingers

Clutching at the living, rounded limbs:

"O do not pass by, stranger, for I

Lie here, unburied and dispersed,

Unhonoured in this sodden meadow,

This field, that was the ground of slaughter.

Unnoticed, I have lain, a century

Of oblivion passing by.

And I have set a snare for you,

Rust-blackened and deep in filth.

You might mistake it for a clod of earth,

But it has the fire of hell within.

Soon you will lie here with me, here

And scattered, dead, dismembered,

Random molecules, unseen.

Your death will be a ceremony

Your blood, a dark libation

Received into this thirsty ground."

Further North

At Alesund

We stopped at Alesund: Jugendstil.

Smart shops, grand houses, a prissy feel.

We drank chocolate in a small café

And climbed a hill to while an hour away.

And from the not too demanding height,

We saw the fjord in a flat grey light.

You slipped and held my hand that day;

Once you would have done it anyway.

We watched the children in a nursery school

Tumbling over in their bright kagools

And as we watched then gambol down a hill,

I thought I saw your eyes begin to fill

At promises unkept, things we had not done,

Hope left unfulfilled, children left unborn.

The Arctic Cathedral

At Tromso, there is a church that stands upon a rock;

A great white fang, jutting into the arctic sky,

Assertive and improbable. There, we heard

A soprano with a choirboy's voice, asexual and clear,

Pour out sad melismas into the anointed light

While a cello warmed with its mellow baritone

The cold and cloistered air. We sat an hour,

No more, and crossed the bridge that sprang

Across the black and sluggish fjord in a blade of light

To where the city huddled in a hollow

Lit with a hail of quiet and frozen stars.

The North Cape

You must remember the skeleton

Of a globe they have there: world

Without flesh, lines of latitude

Embodied, become the whole?

You stood before it, so did I,

Embarrassed at the banality

Of posing in such awful grandeur.

The sea was calm that day, heaving

Like a restless bed, sluggish

And replete. Wildness had forsaken

Its imperium for an hour. Yet,

I felt the call of it, could understand

Why Nansen left his ship to walk

A thousand miles, to where

All journeys meet, and the only way

Is down. Or Amundsen, his nose

As sharp and straight as the blade

Of an executioner, his eyes

Remote and ruthless, burnished

By staring into the gale

For a horizon that never came,

Calculating how many lives

Of dogs and men to spend,

To plant a flag where there is no soil.

Light over the Lofotens

Do you remember the light? The meld
Of dawn into evening, twilight into dawn,
Yellow and red, orange and indigo,
Rising from the horizon like a vision
Of eternity. Turner could have painted it,
And caught the silence it honoured
By its epiphany. The sun you do not see,
But feel its presence there, beyond
The mountains rising from the sea, lying
In its winter bed, gathering its majesty
For the brief, elusive, hoped-for spring.

The return of the Northern people

They had meant them to wait, the cosy men

In heated offices with padded chairs

Cosseting plump backsides, the bureaucrats,

The slide-rule men, the ordered men

Who organize everything and understand

Nothing. They had wanted them to wait

For timber houses and metalled roads,

For schools and sewers and offices

And drains. They did not know, had never felt

The mystery of the sun crouched behind

The edge of the world, like some hesitant,

Awaited guest, never sensed the glamour

Of the final solitude, of being the last

In all the world. And so, they stood and watched,

After the beast had gone, and the people

Came, like reindeer sucking familiar moss,

Men and mothers and babes in arms,

The people of the North, in skins

Of seal and reindeer and Arctic fox,

The people who live off the land,

The people in whom the land lives:

The dark, the cold, the lacerating wind

Their being. They came back when they could,

No need to wait, and lived on the land

And what it bore: in upturned boats

Ramshackle shed, ice-houses, caves.

The memory remains, of death

And resurrection, loss and gain.

Arctic villages

The villages are like jetsam

Straggling the shore,

Having no reason to be there,

But the whim of the sea and the tide,

Their presence tolerated,

Not essential: painted houses,

Slender road, flirting sides

Of echoing fjords, stubborn,

Assertive in their way,

Pitiful under the giant soar

And circle of the eagle who oversees

Sea and sky with black wings,

Aged head and all-consuming eye.

Outside the nursery

We watched the children tumble down the hill

Like small red boulders. In the Northern chill

Their laughing faces flushed, pink as the sky

As dawn melded into twilight. You and I

Stood, wondering at their careless joy,

Their glory in the simple waste of energy,

The rush of wind against unprotected face,

The impetus of a headlong downhill race.

We wondered how our own kids might have raced,

Pink-cagooled and scarlet-faced,

Down the icy hill, if there had been

Kids to set in such a scene.

Together, we might have watched them grow.

As we merely stand and mourn them now.

Arctic Night on Board

The salt wind, onward surge of the sea

Scours the first layer of skin away,

Leaving it rough as pumice. The sea,

Oily, black, sluggish with imaginings,

Glittered. The moon cut a silver furrow,

Lighting the wake with easy radiance.

The Aurora hung bright green cobwebs

On the points of stars. A meteorite fell

A shining path to oblivion. Beside me,

A man put up a tripod as if to sacrifice

A goat, spaniel-like in his flapping fur;

Another, erect, bare-headed, greybeard,

Appeared to weep, tears dragged from him

Like shoots from frozen ground. We stopped

By a jagged ravine, to look for trolls.

A light shone, where no human ought to be,

Leaving us a conjecture, or a mystery.

Other Places

In Ravenna

Ravenna was flat: empty streets
At three in the afternoon, grey skies,
The promise of rain, shirt soaked
To the thinness of a second skin.

We sat outside a restaurant,
Expecting service. No one came.
Inconsequentially, we wandered
Out of the purposeless square.

That morning, we had been
Under a vault of azure sky
Set with golden stars, next
To a red octagonal church.

It reminded me of Byzantium
And was intended to,
A recreation, a new birth
And a reassertion.

Christ in majesty, angels,

Prophets, the imperial family,

The old whore in epiphany,

Burnished in gold, shameless:

Alive. Dead fifteen hundred years

And living in gold leaf

And coloured stone. Outside,

Time lying heavy on red brick.

Leaving Venice

The mist was down; it soaked shirt, skin,

Deleting colour, denying definition.

I stood at the vaporetto stop,

And saw the canal glide a slow turn

Sluggishly, into the obscure. Lights

Glittered like beads of dew, strung

On cobwebs on a winter lawn.

Only the voices of women, young,

American, strident and sharp, cut

Into the silence of the breaking dawn.

Gracelessly, we stirred the black

Stream, lending an unwanted purpose,

A direction, alien to the scene,

Disrupting the still unwoken city,

Battering out into the lagoon,

Past the jutting piles, the gulls

That sit as sentinels, as centuries

Form millennia, unnoticeable,

Irreplaceable, past the blind wall

Of San Michele, past Murano.

And out to sea. We had forgotten

The sea, the tamed, the built-on

Fenced-in, sea, walking those

Fondamente, those sottopassegiate,

Edged in green slime, past windows

Bright with sequinned masks,

Glass beads, mannequins dressed

For Carnevale, crowds of Koreans

Tipped off boats, to wander

Without comprehension, for an hour.

Gaza

A father carries his little daughter

Wrapped up all in white,

Tiny, lifeless, still and light:

The life she had no longer there.

The missiles fall again like rain,

The bodies lie around dismembered,

Sad, bloody, unremembered,

And the children die again.

Again and again they die,

Pathetic scraps in makeshift shrouds,

While all around the bombs sound loud

And merciless in the sky.

Florence and Venice

I used to be a Florence man,

All sobriety and line

And intellect and design,

Pietra serena: perspective, plan,

Grim exteriors, rough facades,

Regulated space, geometry,

A sense of perfect clarity:

No posturing, no parades.

But I have grown into a Venetian,

With all the farts, the seepages,

The exhalations of old age,

The slow subsiding ruin of a man

As of a city: the rotting magnificence

Of crumbling walls and decaying sense.

Accidents and Encounters

Yesterday's meeting

I had seen her sitting there. "A girl,"
I think you called her, after she had gone.
A girl of fifty-four, one who knew you
And you her, neither well. She sat alone,
Behind you, facing me. You were turned
Away. I noticed her, that she was still
A women waiting to be noticed, packed
Unceremoniously into too-tight jeans,
Hair the colour of trodden corn. She caught
My eye a time or two, and looked away,
Thinking perhaps she ought to know me,
But had forgot. Drinking a skinny latte,
She sat alone in the aluminium café,
Among the potted plants, with pairs
Of elderly women set around the room.

She rose to leave, her coffee finished
Fifteen minutes before, and turned to you.

"It's me," she said, and you confirmed it was

In a small impromptu ceremony

Of recognition. She talked awhile,

Stridently, as women do who wish to seem

Alone by choice, recalling people, incidents,

Grown to significance, as islands revealed

By a receding tide. You had been at school

Together, five years apart, Loud and brassy

In her leather coat, her northern vowels

Sharp as spoons clattering against cups,

She spoke of years ago, of youth, of men,

Of pleasures, possibilities unrealised,

Friendships insufficiently explored.

Quickly, with easy censure, I summed her up.

"Common as muck," my mother would have said,

"No better than she ought to be." I never

Understand how anyone can be better

Than they ought to be. All my life had readied

Me not to like her, this woman clutching

On to youth with clinging jeans

And coloured hair. You asked about her bloke,

A husband I dare say. "He had," she said,

"Two 'eart attacks and a stroke when 'e

Were forty-nine. 'e don't get out that much,

But I can leave 'im for an hour or two."

And this she said in words as free

Of bitterness as they were innocent

Of aspirates: life was the way it was.

And so, she left, off to buy some Christmas junk.

I saw her waddling in the distance,

Butting her way through shopping crowds

And coloured lights, stoical and stout.

Curley's saved

Curley's is saved for the nation

And for me. I can take my station

Up there on the hill

And eat my fill

Of overcooked bacon, greasy batter,

And other decaying matter.

Or sit on the terrace in the last light

And watch the afternoon

Decline into the night,

And follow the swallows' flight

Low over the lake

When summer comes again

And the far-off rumoured sea

Is a radiance, white

In the early evening sky

Seen from there on high

On Curley's terrace on the hill.

Doing something with yourself

I met a woman I had not seen,
Perhaps, for half a year. Afriend?
Yes, if a woman can be a friend.
Thin strands of affection hung
Across the distances between us,
Like bunting across a street.

Quickly, she said where she had been
And why, and to what end, furiously
Crossing the bewildered world
On long-spun vapour trails
Describing arabesques
Between continents across the sky.

She complained of weariness.
Indeed, she seemed thinner
Than she had been, the skin
Hanging like crumpled paper

On her upper arms, her chin

Tauter than before, and grim.

As I contemplated the change

In her, wondering what difference

She saw in me: rounder, yes,

And content, she might have thought,

Fuller faced; she paused and asked,

"But come on, what of you?

What have you been doing with yourself?"

"Doing," I thought, "What is there

I should have done, what self

Is it that you mean?" Silent, I sat,

Struggling to recall the months

That had passed me, unregarding, by.

There was nothing I remembered,

Nothing I wanted to recall,

Only a time of slow accretion,

Gathering dust, declining years.

Was this, I wondered, happiness?

Perhaps it is all there is.

Bertie

My cat is giving me an appraising stare.

You'd think there was intelligence there.

There isn't really, you know.

It only looks as though it might be so.

His toughest problem on any day

Is finding the location of the litter tray.

He may look as though he's wrestling with a poser,

You may mistake him for a furry-faced Spinoza,

But the only puzzle on his mind

Is where to park his great big soft behind.

A distant bird

I thought I heard a buzzard's cry,

Distant, plaintive and effete.

Itself I could not see.

It was somewhere where the clouds meet,

Secret, tenebrous and high,

Spooling round its winding circle

The filaments of sky:

The threads you cannot see

That bind the everlasting sky

To the accidental earth

As the aeons meander by.

It was a bird I heard,

Sharp as acid in the sky,

Winding circles in and out

In his own immensity.

A defiant teenager

The kitten purrs on your lap,

The puppy rolls over; the small child

Climbs into your bed, the old lady

Sends a card. The schoolboy

Stands defiant, thuggish

And sixteen, anxieties

Buzzing in his brain

Like mosquitos on a summer night.

He wants what the kitten wants

Or the dog or the old lady

Or himself twelve years before.

But he cannot purr,

Display his tender parts,

Express his vulnerabilities

By gesture or in words.

He can merely say, "I'm a shit.

Love me in spite of it."

The Couple

They passed me on the sloping path

That passes Yarrow and the Lead Mines Clough;

Something they would not have done

A dozen years ago. They did not hear

My quiet "Good Morning." I did not

Mean them to; the wind conspired with me,

Granting me inaudibility, as my age

Made certain I would not be seen:

A man, a girl, bright in their T-shirts,

Despite the trace of winter in the wind.

They would make love that day, or perhaps

Already had, and walked, not for exercise,

Or diet, or to recapture memory,

But for the exhilaration of the wind,

The song of birds, the early promises

Of spring. She gripped his hand tightly

To assist her on the sharply cobbled

Path, pointing and, with laughter, speech

And gesture, conducting their small ensemble.

He said little, seeming from behind

To acquiesce. I wonder if it crept

Into his mind to question, as in mine,

At what point, and how, her need

Became his obligation

The Marian Consort

Sandstone and intricate:

The tower an aspiration

And an assertion, Somerset

Ecclesiastical, C of E

In every detail of its filigree.

Packed that night, inside

And out, gravestones soft

And scoured, names mostly gone,

One restored: a name, rank, VC,

A hero gone to modest glory.

Inside, Rear-Admirals,

Colonels, Brigadiers,

Resting patient haunches

On unyielding Victorian pews

Giving God his uncomplaining dues.

In harmonious complication,

Its own unassuming filigree,

The music rises in blended voices,

Sweet in the clustered air.

A bird echoes it, somewhere.

The Museum Instinct

I struggle to catch the moment,

To capture and tidy it away,

Like a specimen in a jar,

Like a shrunken head,

Like a fly in amber,

Like the shell of an egg

From which a boy has sucked the yoke,

As a kitten tries to catch a butterfly,

As clouds try to catch the moon,

As a lover tries to catch a glimpse,

As the widow tries to catch an echo

At the unresponding grave.

There is nothing that can be caught,

Nothing to be filed away,

No moments to be preserved,

No life in the empty shell.

A pratfall in Aylesbury

If you want to fall flat on your face,

Aylesbury is just the place.

It was excellent for me;

I recommend Aylesbury.

They provide pavements there,

They have them everywhere.

They hide under the municipal grass

To tap your ankles as you pass.

And so, you fall spectacularly from grace,

Head long forward on your face,

With time only to emit,

The cry, as I did, "shit!"

Mr.Gove

The voice minces across its vowels

Like a girl, first time in high heels

On cobbles in a gale, careful,

Prissy, anxious not to slip. The words

Are elegant, precisely picked, arranged

Like lilies in a vase. The Secretary

Speaks well, commands the House,

Sends forth his Latinate squadrons

Into the ever watchful ether, to resound

In millions of closed minds. Only

The most uncharitable will observe

That his erudition means no more

Than the whimper of a dreaming dog

Or the passage of wind

Through tightly clamped cheeks.

Boff

Boff was in again today, peddling

Maniacally away, his beer belly

Poised like an anxious pelican

Over his lycra shorts. He is bald now,

Except for tufts of hair like ears

On a koala bear: bald and amiable

And pink with effort, legs pumping,

Cheeks billowing, mouth gaping,

Not speaking, though he will be soon;

He is not a man for silence, Boff.

His advice is freely given, whether sought

Or not, and he is prodigal

With information. He used

To be a policeman, suspicious deaths

His speciality, investigating, not

Inflicting. The things he saw

He will not tell, too terrible

For speech, too repellent

To be recalled. Once again,

He is a copper on his bike, going

Nowhere, safely in the gym.

A Conversation with Lee James

He had his flowers, his cat,

His telly, his council flat;

He wasn't very quick.

He may have been a little thick.

Tell me, tell me why

Mr Ebrahimi had to die.

He was scum, a weirdo,

A darkie and a paedo

A bloody Pak

From somewhere in Iraq.

And that is why

The bastard had to die.

He wasn't very strong.

It won't have taken very long

To hurl him to the ground

With your mates around

And kick him in the head,

Making sure that he was dead.

No, I enjoyed that bit.

Watched him rolling in the shit,

Stuck my foot

Into ribs and gut,

Kicked and kicked him in the head

Even after he was dead.

And did you feel no shame

No sense of blame

At spilling helpless blood?

Did it perhaps feel good

To kill with hands and feet

In the quiet street?

Yeah, it felt alright.

I went home that night,

Thinking we had it sorted,

Proud of what I did,

Killed the filthy sod

Like an avenging god.

And so we lit,

My mates and me, a fire

And burned the little shit

Watched the flames leap higher.

And now the streets are free

For decent folk like you and me.

No Greater Happiness

I remembered, as the breeze

Ruffled the meadow, soft as a kiss,

Many, many days, and thought

There is no greater happiness than this.

I remembered, how in the meadow

You greeted me with a kiss

Many, many times, and thought

There was no greater happiness than this.

And now it is only left to me

To remember the meadow and the kiss,

Though we move towards December,

There is no greater happiness than this.

Harold

My uncle Harold prophesied doom.

It was his hobby,

His way of dispelling gloom.

"Armageddon was on its way,"

He would smile and say. It said

It in the Bible, which he had not read

And in the Watchtower, which he had.

It never seemed to make him sad:

The approaching conflagration,

The moral decline of the British nation,

The inevitable relegation

Of his football team,

Which he did not watch, in a town

He did not see any more,

Since he never left his room

At the end, smiling in the gloom

At the rapidly approaching doom

Of the human race, the nation,

The approaching conflagration,

The inevitable relegation.

Gym Talk

Two young women, adjoining,

Matching stride for stride

In the insistent rhythm

Of the machine. Once, they would

Have stood together in a mill;

Now they sweat for vanity

Or to keep a husband.

They find, as I do not,

The breath to speak, legs

Pumping, clutching arms

Retaining balance on the

Spinning tread. They speak

In a kind of polyphony,

Voices intermingling, intent.

It is hard not to listen,

And you do, there being nothing

Else to speed the minutes

You impose upon yourself.

They speak of children,

Putting them to bed, waking them,

Feeding, getting them to school.

They are beautiful, these girls,

Glistening with honest sweat,

Cheeks red with effort, bodies

Sleek with youth, their voices

Northern, assertive, loud:

And yet, nothing better

Than motherhood to occupy their talk.

Still, I thought, as I worked away,

Listening half enviously,

What should better be than this,

The careful moulding of a life,

The tasks that spin the fabric

Of the years from the slender silk

Of childhood's fragile day.

An Evasion

I thought I saw, or seemed to see,

In the supermarket store, a woman who used to be

Beautiful, or so I thought, and so did she.

But she pretended not to see

And I pretended not to be

The man I was, or that I meant to be.

I turned away, and so did she,

Preoccupied, or seeming so to be.

Why, I find impossible to see.

And so, perhaps, did she.

Being careful

There once was a man who avoided risk.

He sat in his house wearing a mask,

With padlocks on the doors

And plastic sheeting on the floors.

The windows were shuttered;

The medicine shelf cluttered;

There were rails on the stairs

And dozens of pairs

Of crutches, just in case,

And Factor sixty for his face,

Though he never went out

And was never seen about

Without wearing a mac

And rucksack on his back

With emergency supplies

Of food, medicine; all that was wise.

Having no dog or cat or wife,

He sat all alone, saving his life.

In the Cafe

A line of women, queuing for tea,
Skinny latte, cappuccino, filter coffee,
Risking perhaps an Eccles cake or scone,
Few of them, like me, alone.

It was busier, I thought, yesterday.
The rain has kept the shoppers away,
Sweeping in from the west.
These are the times I like the best.

Times when I sit, unobserved, alone,
Hiding behind my paper, no one
Caring whether I am there or not,
A harmless old bloke, wholly forgot.

Women in pairs, queuing for tea,
None known, none knowing me.
I watch them, merely because I can,
No threat to them, just an old man.

Love?

I wonder if my cat loves me.
Sometimes, I think he might.
Sometimes, I think you do, too.
Both cannot be right.

He looks at me, with what might be
A gleam of adoration
Or, more probably,
Incipient starvation.

He rolls over on his back
As once you used to do,
Purring idiotically
As you did one day, too.

I suppose that I shall never know
What he thinks of me.
My fear is that you might possibly
Resolve that ambiguity.

Memory

Closed, the book looks solid, handsome,

Armoured in thick dark brown leather

Soldier-like, within a rank of like

Infantry. It breathes dependability;

It will stand you close, guard your side,

Protect everything you hold most dear.

But it is old, the book, fragile

Within, as wings of butterflies,

Two days dead. You must not turn

The cover, ruffle the pages,

Expose the ink to the bright light

And importunity of the day.

All you thought it held will fall away,

Crumble into molecules of dust,

Dead cells to spiral in the sun,

And with it, you: you the mighty

The unconquerable, fading,

Dry, easy as a leaf to break

In the first autumnal frost.

A Few Grumbles

Active waists

"Active waists:" that's what I need.

Trousers with a hidden band

That yields as I expand

Sympathetic to my greed.

I must avoid exposure to a glass,

Reflection does nothing to enhance

The struggle of my pants

To encompass the spreading of my ass.

I need not admit to being stout:

The trousers take the strain

And the slender youth that lies within

Can succeed in getting out.

First Time

I thought you would remember the day we met,

But it has slipped beyond recall;

And if I ask, "did you notice me?"

You reply, too honestly, "not at all."

Yet, you see, I do remember the first

Time I ever saw you, what you said, where we were.

You had a kind of melancholy about you,

We were in a bar; smoke softened your hair

From the cigarette you held. You spoke

Of having met a man an hour or two before,

And been amused. "An interesting bloke,"

I think you said. " He spoke of an affair.

And of the girl with whom he was having it.

He seemed strangely fond of her."

You did not see, because you had not noticed me

By then, how your observation left me poised

Between compassion and jealousy,

Optimism and regret: so young to be

So painfully aware of the tendency of love

To turn into its opposite or, worse,

To nothingness, the absence thereof.

I wondered what had led you to

This premature maturity,

And whether there was hope in it,

But still, you did not notice me.

Barclays

Millions are cheated, profits fall,

Thousands of workers get the boot

But all the bosses – I do mean all –

Get bonuses. Can you work it out?

They need to retain talent, you see:

The talent that engineered the fall

And earned the workers redundancy.

Most of us would shoot them all.

Can you believe it? Nor can I

The government can. I wonder why.

O2 be in England

O to be other than O2:

The cell that closes

In the lee of a hill

Or the shadow of a tree,

Or near a building

Or by a wall.

Why have the thing at all?

Do you remember silence,

Comforting, profound and deep:

Silence unbroken by a bell,

Vulgarized Mozart,

Invaders from outer space

Or half-remembered tunes

From forgotten films?

We had leisure then:

To read, to think,

To walk, to sniff the air,

To make love, or think

Of making love.

Instead, we have:

Coitus interruptus,

Expensive tinnitus

In unwilling ears,

No privacy,

The prison of

Unlimited accessibility.

And, if I want to make a call,

The bloody thing

Won't work at all.

Flight 370

They let them know by text, it seems.

That's how we do it now. No more

The solemn Copper, the nice hot cup of tea,

The embarrassed neighbour, wondering how

To cook the dinner, collect the kids,

Stay sane in this miasma of circling

Grief. That's not how we do it now.

"Malaysian Airlines regrets to announce"

What? That it has deposited flesh

Of your flesh, blood of your blood

On the ocean bed, two miles deep,

Where the sun can never reach, as far

From possibility of recovery or recall

As Jupiter. But they have sent a text,

Replete with dignity and regret. They will

Have thought about it long and hard,

Set up a committee, to protect the brand.

These things do not just happen. They

Have a reputation to protect. Most

Of the bereaved, are, when all

Is said and done, Chinese, they

Do not feel things the way we do.

There are so many of them; too many

To grieve for them all. The woman

I saw rush wild-eyed, screaming,

From the ornate hotel, her life cancelled,

Past and future both made null, son

And grandson lost, as though never

Having lived, seemed not to understand

Her ethnic incapacity for grief.

She was screaming for her son.

They only allow them one.

My Absence

It will not much matter to the hills.

The sheep that pare them down

Are different sheep; the booted feet

That mark the contour lines are not

The same, and are no different.

The clouds that drift across the changing,

Unchanging surface of the lake

Are the same, and not the same.

The water in the clough will sing

The same unharmonious clatter

Over the same pebbles. The sky

Will change at every moment

And remain the same; the falcon

Will circle slowly with the same

Indifference, wrapt in mastery,

The aristocracy of the assassin.

The sea will still be there, rising

And falling in the rhythm of the tide.

Nothing changes, and everything does.

A man dies, and is not renewed:

Once expended, life does not return:

A peck of ashes, a modest cloud:

Our petty pawn of matter

At last redeemed, nothing changes

And change itself goes on, unchanged.

Bedding plants

Bedding plants in today,

Back aching, nails full of dirt

But still a better way

Of hurrying summer along

Than cutting the throat

Of a priest, or burning

The entrails of a goat

On a tripod. Resting

On my spade, I survey,

Across the valley beneath

The passing of the day

From dark to final dark.

Management Training

"Write down," he says, "Without thinking, what the words

Written on your card mean to you. Don't tell anyone"

Secretly, I turn my card around. "Autumn leaves," it says.

Glancing around, I write: "Literary trope: metaphor

For human mortality." I stop. Everyone continues

Writing. Should I add some more? There is nothing

Left to say. "Who had autumn leaves?" he asks.

Six hands are raised reluctantly like stalks emerging

Into a frozen spring. A woman in a low cut sweater

With pointed nipples snagging on merino wool

Reads: "Autumn leaves are very pretty. They are red

And brown and yellow; they crunch beneath your feet."

A man replies: "Autumn leaves are a bloody pest.

They block your drains and rot hideously on your lawn."

Another offers: "Autumn leaves, but not soon enough.

Winter is to be preferred. You know where you are

In winter." A girl then says, "Autumn leaves are old

And withered. Like some people, they hang around

Too long."Then it is my turn. I get a slight

Embarrassed laugh, a collective focussing

Of curious stares. I am, I realize, an oddity.

Revealing nothing, I have given myself away.

Going to the airport

She will go tomorrow, with the light;

When the day unwraps itself and starts

To rise, when the blackbird starts to sing

Across the lingering silence. She

Will smile goodbye, lifting unsteadily

The case I will not be there to bear,

Worrying at her passport, boarding card,

Irritating detritus of departure,

Usually left to me. She will say,

"Six days, only six, not quite a week.

Not much to ask. Before you know it,

I'll be back." Six, but what proportion

Of all the days that are left is that?

And I shall wish her well, and drive away,

Swallowing the fear that rises, acid in my throat.

Woken by cats

I was late again today. Sleep
Would not let go of me; the quilt
Wrapped itself around me,
Gravity was too much to bear;
Light intruded and deceived.
It could not be, must not be
Morning. At the bottom of the bed
Sat the cats, staring in identical
Hostility, dignified and aggrieved,
In an attitude of accusation.
"Breakfast is late, my man,"
They clearly, silently, said,
Unblinking, relentless and assured.
And so I rose, accepting wearily
The first defeat of the morning.

No Lance

Lance was ill again today. Not there,

Rumoured to be getting worse;

Not seen, last heard of weeks ago,

Last heard from when last seen.

Without him, there is silence,

No unceasing hum of words

Emitted without thought of meaning:

Words that fill spaces, make bridges

Over emptiness, that spring from strength,

Contented absorption in

The contemplation of self, words

That, without meaning, still express

A soul, not quiet, but at peace,

Drawing others in with a warmth

Virile, gentle and self-sustained.

I fear I may not see again

The battered asymmetry of his face,

His elephant legs, purple with veins

Burst and prominent, his head

That sits upon his shoulders

Like a rock upon a summit cairn.

The Financial Adviser

She did not speak of death, you see.

She used the word, "mortality:"

Mine, then somewhat later, yours

Allotting us more years,

Perhaps than fate would allocate,

Assigning each of us a date

Remote enough to reassure.

But still the word was there,

On the page, final as the stroke

That severs head from neck.

You need to plan, you see

To the limit of mortality.

Smiling, she advised us,

Clotho, Lachesis and Atropos

In one. And now, we look ahead

To when we shall both be dead.

Lightning Source UK Ltd.
Milton Keynes UK
UKOW02f1814161216
290160UK00001B/27/P